CUSTOMER TESTIMONIALS
FOR
FUN AND PROFIT

JOHN WILLOUGHBY

Copyright © 2018 John Willoughby

All Rights Reserved

ISBN: 9781792888397

Table of Contents

1	THE VALUE OF CUSTOMER TESTIMONIALS	1
2	PSYCHOLOGY OF INFLUENCE	5
3	TESTIMONIALS TO DRIVE PROLIFERATION	13
4	COLLECTING TESTIMONIALS	21
5	VIDEO TESTIMONIALS: DOING IT RIGHT	32
6	SHOOTING YOUR OWN VIDEO	36
7	USING SMARTPHONES	49
8	TRADE-SHOW INTERVIEWS	54
9	RELEASE FORMS	58
10	USING THE TESTIMONIALS	60
11	CONCLUSION	67

1 THE VALUE OF CUSTOMER TESTIMONIALS

Rare is the child who was not, at least once, treated to the age-old question *If everyone else jumped off a cliff, would you?* And no doubt you probably just rolled your eyes or snorted and walked off. It's a rhetorical question, and no reply was really expected.

Of course, you are not going to do something silly just because your friends do it. Because you are not a "sheep". You do not blindly follow the herd. You are an individual, in control of your destiny, and you do only what you want to do. If you do jump off that cliff, it will be because that is what you want to do, not because anyone else did it.

I always thought the whole cliff-jumping thing was a silly way for my parents to try to trick me out of doing exciting things. If I was going to do something that everyone else was doing, that was just because we all appreciated the same cool things that my parents just didn't get.

And anyway, I grew up in the Midwest, which has very flat land, and the threat of cliff jumping seemed pretty remote at best. There just weren't any cliffs for many miles, although that kind of missed the whole point of the story, didn't it?

Unfortunately, it turns out that we all have a bit of the sheep in us. And that includes your customers. We can't help ourselves; it's just programmed into us. It's who we are in our bones. If everyone else was jumping off a cliff, would we? Well, yes. Maybe not literally, but in most cases we would metaphorically jump.

There are times when following the crowd isn't such a bad thing. We learn from others both consciously and unconsciously. This lets us acquire the wisdom of the herd without having to try out everything ourselves. This can be extremely useful when it involves potentially dangerous situations. Learning from the group can save us from having to learn a fatal lesson.

We might not know the roar of a lion ourselves, but maybe some others in our tribe recognize it and tell us it's time to run. We might not have seen first-hand that some berries are poisonous, but others in the tribe have seen people die after eating them and they tell us about it.

On the other hand, even the collective wisdom of the group can let us down at times, and then we suffer by taking action based on faulty information. And we do unfortunate things. Like jumping off that cliff.

To be fair, a lot of cliff jumping is the result of having incomplete information. In the absence of facts to rely on, we will turn to the wisdom of the herd as a source of information because that's better than no information, right?

I may not have experienced something myself, but someone else may have, and this is what they learned from their experience. I don't have to experience everything firsthand; I just need to acquire the herd's collective knowledge. I might not have used a product myself, but it gets good reviews on Amazon so it's probably ok.

On the surface, it seems that this is a good practice. If everyone else is doing something, can it really be wrong? With so many people contributing their experience and knowledge, the group wisdom surely must be right. Except that when we take a closer look, we find that group wisdom is rarely based on the experience of everyone in the group, or even of a majority of the people in the group.

In fact, it turns out that convention can be started by a very small number of people. This means that we really don't even need to wait for everyone to be jumping off a cliff to motivate us to jump. It only takes a few people to get things started. And when group wisdom is set not by the group but by a few individuals, we need to consider exactly how wise is the group wisdom in any particular situation. Just because two people believe the same thing that doesn't mean it's right.

From the perspective of a marketer, this is actually great news. In order to influence someone to buy our product, we don't have to prove to them that *everyone* else is using it, merely that a representative handful of people are using it. This is why customer stories and testimonials are so important, despite being so often neglected.

I will also note here that I will generally use the term *customer testimonial*. There are many different forms of testimonials, and many different titles that are given to describe them. Whether it is a customer success story, customer quote, customer endorsement, customer recommendation, or some other title, the end result is the same. The customer is giving you an endorsement in one form or another, and that makes it a testimonial. For simplicity's sake, that is the term I will use in this book.

> To influence someone to buy your product you don't have to prove that *everyone* else is using it, merely that a representative handful of people are using it.

2 PSYCHOLOGY OF INFLUENCE

Why do customer testimonials work? Most people agree that customer testimonials are a component in building product and service credibility with new prospects. No one would say that a customer testimonial is a bad thing. Generally, an important factor for any good product evaluation is the success that other customers have had with the product and whether or not they were satisfied enough to actually recommend the product.

A lot of marketing is based on experience and what is often referred to as *gut feel*. We re-use techniques that have worked in the past, we incorporate customer feedback into our plans, and we get ideas from watching what other companies do. But making the most effective use of our resources requires that we look a little deeper and actually analyze the basis for our activities.

How are customer testimonials helpful? When and how should they be used? How many are needed? These are questions that can be answered by turning to studies in social psychology on exactly how people are influenced by others.

The Basics: Reducing Perceived Risk

A basic reason for providing customer testimonials is to help reduce the perceived risk of purchasing your product. If other customers are willing to state, in public, that they were successful with the product, then that is one more checkmark on the list of due-diligence tasks that a potential customer will make.

A customer testimonial by itself might not convince the prospect that your product is perfect, but the absence of them speaks volumes. If you went to Amazon and saw some product that had no reviews, you'd assume that no one had used it yet. Why would you want to be the first one to take a chance on it, or worse, why would you buy something that obviously no one else thought was good enough to purchase?

In this respect, customer testimonials are a critical component to guarantee a successful evaluation. They may or may not provide a positive benefit by their presence, but their absence definitely provides a negative one. More testimonials mean more successful customers which means the perception of less risk in purchasing the product.

Another benefit of a customer testimonial is that it provides examples of how other customers have used your product, and in what situations. This makes it a part of your documentation as a sales tool and helps show people how they will be successful using your product.

Using Social Proof

Moving beyond being a mere checkmark on a list of evaluation tasks, however, the use of customer testimonials really can change customer behavior and attitude. People are, in fact, strongly influenced by the group around them.

There are numerous studies that have shown that individuals can even be influenced to behave in ways that seem contrary to their normal reasoning and beliefs. This can happen because of the behavior of those around them, and all the more so where those exhibiting the behavior are considered to be in some position of authority or having special knowledge or expertise.

Psychologists refer to this as *social proof*, or *informational social influence*. This is a phenomenon where people take on the actions of others around them in order to act with the perceived correct behavior in a situation.

Social proof is particularly present when there is ambiguity in a social situation and individuals are not able to figure out what the correct behavior is on their own. They assume that the crowd around them has more collective knowledge than they do about whatever current situation they are in. In short: herd behavior.

Further, this means that the group can settle on a specific choice quickly and without really any solid foundation at all. A small number of people settle on one idea, and the group around them picks this up, and then more people see them and pick it up and so on. It's like a chain reaction, and this is referred to as an *information cascade*.

Social proof can be used to drive conformity and change people's behavior or beliefs in response to the actions of others. Other people's comments and actions act as a source of information about what is right and wrong.

> **Social Psychology** is the study of how the thoughts, feelings, and behaviors of individuals are influenced by the actual, imagined, or implied presence of others.

Early experiments by the psychologist Muzafer Sherif, one of the founders of social psychology, first explored this principle. Social influence is particularly important where the correct answer is not completely clear, such as when two products have similar characteristics or a similar array of pros and cons.

Even more interesting, in experiments conducted by the psychologist Solomon Asch, it was shown that a surprisingly high percentage of people will conform to group opinions even where that opinion conflicts with their own, original beliefs.

Many of us can remember badgering our parents for some toy or to see some movie because all of our friends had seen it or bought it and we felt hopelessly left out. The fact that all of our friends had an experience denied to us often became the primary reason we wanted it so badly.

If everyone else was jumping off a cliff, would you? Asch's studies showed that yes, in fact, many people actually would. Not everyone, of course, but many. Perhaps we would not actually jump off a cliff, but we do feel a strong compulsion to go along with the crowd. It has nothing to do with what the crowd is doing, merely that the crowd is doing it and, as social animals ourselves, we feel a compulsion to also engage in similar behavior.

Clearly, the existence of good customer testimonials can influence the prospective customer's perception of the product. This is distinct from the basic evaluation checkmark and actually has nothing to do with the fact that others are using the product successfully, merely that others are using the product. They wouldn't be using it if the product was bad, would they? Of course not! Or so we think.

How Many Testimonials Are Enough?

Having determined that the customer testimonial is an important part of a marketing strategy, we need some idea of how many stories we need to have in order to be effective. There is, of course, a cost of obtaining each new testimonial, so we want to make sure we have enough but not waste resources by having more than we need.

Further studies by Asch were conducted to investigate exactly how many social references are required to change the behavior of an individual who is in a group setting.

By examining experiments where the behavior of an individual is being swayed by a crowd and then varying the number of people who are trying to convince the individual to change their mind, we can get some insight into the number of references that are required.

For example, if a group of people are all predisposed to make a certain choice and some of the members of the group begin arguing for a different choice, how many people need to make the argument before the group begins to be swayed in their new choice? If one person argues for a different choice, is that enough to make the change? Is two enough? Three? More?

Asch showed that it only requires three people making an argument for a specific choice to have a significant impact on the members of a group. The amount of influence increases from one to three people making the statement, and levels off after that. Applying this to the case of customer testimonials, we can deduce that three or four testimonials are adequate to help influence the target customer's preferences.

Of course, they have to be three or four referring customers that the target customer identifies with. The nature of this will vary by industry, and the objective is not necessarily to have a reference that is an exact match for the target customer, but at least one that is using the product or service is generally the same way.

For example, a customer using a computer for business applications might not be a good match when trying to influence someone who wants a computer for gaming. Someone using a computer for word processing, however, might be an acceptable reference for someone who wants to primarily use it for presentations.

That means that you don't need just three customer testimonials, you need three customer testimonials for each major market segment that you are targeting. Otherwise they might be dismissed as simply not relevant. If I read a review of someone using a hammer as a paperweight that doesn't really tell me anything about how it works as a hammer.

And note that since we are trying to influence the customers, these need to be segments that _they_ identify with. Not ones that _you_ think they belong in—ones _they_ think they belong in. It doesn't matter whether you think a car owner should identify with a testimonial from a truck driver, it only matters whether or not the car owner thinks so.

B2B Influence

Much more has been written about using social psychology in consumer marketing than in business-to-business (B2B) marketing. In consumer marketing, where individual preferences make such a large difference in purchasing behavior, the use of techniques like this can make or break a sale all by itself.

In B2B marketing, there are often technical criteria that form the backbone of any purchasing decision. In a business environment, good marketing can rarely overcome a really bad product.

Good marketing can, however, make a dramatic difference where two products both have pros and cons but are similar. As many technical markets face increasing commoditization, these consumer-brand techniques can be quite helpful in the B2B space as well.

Part of the success of B2B marketing is based on your ability to identify your differentiators and to convince your target customers that those specific factors are more important to them than those where your product is weaker.

It is in this situation in particular that techniques like the use of testimonials can make a significant difference in the customer's opinions, or at least keep you from being at a disadvantage when your competition is using these techniques effectively. Unless you hold a patent on some new technology that your customers already believe they can't live without, success or failure of your product is going to rest heavily on the success or failure of your marketing effort.

3 DRIVING PROLIFERATION

Beyond using customer testimonials to help drive new prospects to purchase, there is another useful aspect to these stories: helping to drive proliferation and customer loyalty. Obtaining a customer testimonial can be just as important to promote existing customer retention as it is to help acquire new customers.

Using a testimonial within the same company is something that is sometimes overlooked in marketing programs in the absence of any specific targeted campaign for proliferation. But the customer testimonial can be an important tool in retaining the customer who contributes the story, and even expanding proliferation within that particular customer.

Because it comes from someone within a company, the author of the testimonial has a high degree of credibility within that company and that makes it a highly useful tool to convince others within the same company to also buy your product or service.

Using a testimonial as a highly credible tool within the same company makes sense, but there is another use for it that people often don't realize: making existing customers even more loyal.

Creating lifelong customers

A core discovery about how humans behave is that we will actually change our beliefs to match our actions. Yes, our actions are generally driven by our beliefs in the first place, but when we do something that is not in complete accordance with our current beliefs, we will often resolve the discrepancy by actually changing our opinions. "Yes, I did that because I like to do that." This resolves the internal conflict presented by having our actions diverge from our beliefs.

This is part of the effect of the cognitive dissonance theory developed by the social psychology pioneer Leon Festinger. He discovered that people are troubled by inconsistencies between their thoughts, sentiments, and actions. A state known as *dissonance* occurs when there is a conflict, and this motivates action in order to restore the consistency.

Most of the time, people will act in accordance with their beliefs, so there is no conflict. In cases where they have not acted in complete accordance with their beliefs, however, Festinger realized that they will often actually change their beliefs to resolve the dissonance since they can't go back and change their actions. This is a very important finding, and it means that, simply put, in the case where you can influence someone's actions you can actually change their opinions.

CUSTOMER TESTIMONIALS FOR FUN AND PROFIT

One important caveat for this is that the action must be public or at least leave strong evidence. If we can resolve a conflict between thoughts and actions by simply ignoring or forgetting about the action, we will do so. If we have done something in public or written something down it becomes difficult to simply ignore that action.

That is the situation where we will then be left with the modification of our beliefs as the only solution to resolve the discrepancy and therefore the dissonance. Obviously, the stronger our original inclination, the easier it is to cement a particular belief. If we like a product and end up on the news using that product, we will end up feeling even more positive about the product because of the public commitment.

One place that this impacts us is in the use of customer testimonials. A customer who likes a product well enough to have purchased it and used it once, but might not really love it, can be turned into a more solid customer if you can get them to endorse your product publicly. Obviously if it is good enough to stand up for in public, it must be a wonderful product and one that has been extremely useful for the customer. The customer then modifies what may have been a moderate attraction toward the product to a stronger attraction. This justifies their public action.

CUSTOMER TESTIMONIALS FOR FUN AND PROFIT

Collecting customer testimonials is useful to build product credibility, and that is the main drive behind any such action, but we also get the extra benefit of firmly entrenching the customer's attraction to the product and therefore driving repeat business and internal proliferation. In most businesses, the majority of sales come from existing customers. In addition, the cost of a sale to an existing customer is dramatically lower than the cost to acquire a new customer.

Customers will probably be selected in broad groups to get a spread of representation from different market segments, or by use of specific features, or via other criteria. Beyond that broad grouping, however, our natural inclination is pick the friendliest customers we know to give us the endorsement.

Of course, we feel that will be the easiest way to get such an endorsement and particularly because, no doubt, we enjoy working with them. We know they'll answer our phone call, and we fell like we have a relationship established that let's us ask them for a favor. It's easy and non-threatening for us to make that call.

In light of our understanding of how beliefs and actions are resolved, however, we may want to rethink our strategy for customer selection and focus instead on customers who are friendly enough to work with but not the ones who are completely committed to the product.

By utilizing these marginal customers for endorsements, we can help to turn them into more firmly committed consumers. It may take a bit more effort to get them to agree, but in the end we will have not only a good customer testimonial but also have directly increased customer satisfaction and driven increased proliferation and repeat business.

The Danger of Customer Rewards

Most people will feel an obligation to reward a customer for their participation in the testimonial. This is due to reciprocity. Reciprocity is part of the glue that holds the social fabric together and is seen in primitive animal groups as well as among humans.

In fact, money is itself simply an abstracted form of reciprocity. I do something for you, and you give me an IOU in the form of money. The need to reciprocate is a fundamental part of normal human behavior. When a customer has spent the time to write an endorsement or videotape an interview and is willing to put their name on it publicly, we feel a need to do something nice for them in return.

Certainly, we may feel grateful to them, and showing our appreciation is important to acknowledge their efforts and to be polite. But what we give in exchange can be a critical factor in the effectiveness of the endorsement as part of the customer commitment and our desire to reward them can undermine our efforts.

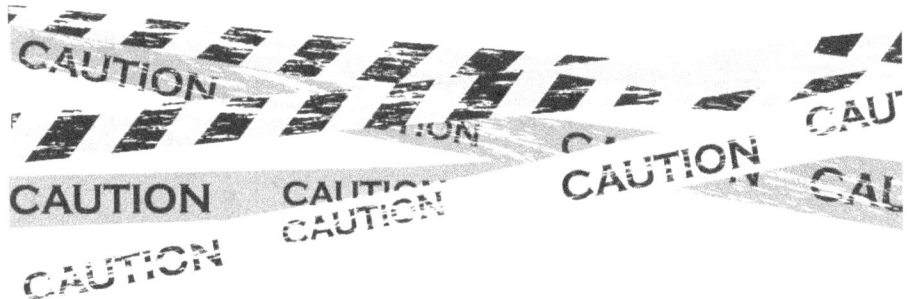

Contrary what we might think initially, the larger the gift as a reward the less effective the endorsement is for helping to commit that customer. We might at first think that the larger the gift the more the customer will be thrilled with us and become an even more ardent supporter. In fact, the exact opposite happens.

Further experiments by Festinger showed that when the subject was rewarded for their original inconsistent behavior, the reward itself gave the participant an out and eliminated the cognitive dissonance without the need to change their opinions. When a customer commits to a product endorsement without thought of reward, this programs them to be a stronger supporter of that product because they rationalize their action by further cementing their attraction to the product.

However, when they receive a valuable reward in exchange for their actions, the result instead is that they subconsciously rationalize their endorsement by the receipt of the gift. Instead of "I did it because I love the product," they instead think "I did it because of the gift I received." This negates the value of the endorsement as a means to increase their attraction to the product.

By all means, show your appreciation. Yes, do give them a gift. But make sure it is a token item without any real value. Don't worry: they gave you the endorsement because they love the product, or because they want the attention, or for any of several other reasons. Getting a free iPad in return was not one of them. Of course, this assumes that you didn't entice them in the first place with an offer of some large reward.

Bribery is rarely an effective technique in any case. You probably can't offer them something large enough to actually get them to endorse a product that they really don't want to endorse, so all you are doing is actually hurting their attraction to the product. There are many reasons why a customer will be willing to provide an endorsement and dangling a free gift in front of them is rarely going to make any difference in whether or not they decide to do it.

Should You Even Ask?

In most corporate settings, the sales team will often be hesitant to let you ask their customer for a testimonial. They worry that you will upset the customer, or confuse a deal in progress, or even dilute their own personal relationship with the customer.

In practice, none of these fears are real problems. I have asked a good many customers to do testimonials, and I have never had a customer have a negative reaction to the request. True, anything is possible, but it is highly unlikely.

Some customers will be thrilled to do it because they get some publicity and it makes them feel important. Some might do it just because they like you or your company and just want to help out. And yes, there are some who will say "no".

Some customers won't want to be interviewed, especially on camera, and they will politely decline. Some customers will want to but can't because of company policies. There are a variety of reasons why they might not say "yes".

But whether or not they agree to be interviewed for the testimonial, they will be polite in their reply. The request will certainly not interfere in any way with the ongoing salesperson–customer relationship. And if the customer does agree, then you have helped secure your relationship even further. There is simply no risk or downside to asking. They won't bite your head off. Well, usually.

The one special case is when you stumble upon an angry customer. This can happen for a variety of reasons, and it's actually not a bad thing. No, it's not going to be much fun for you, but it gives the customer a chance to vent and helps uncover a hidden problem.

You probably won't get an interview out of it, but it will help you identify and begin to fix the problem and retain an at-risk customer. Wouldn't you rather find that out by asking for a testimonial instead of when it's time to renew your contract or purchase order with them? Finding an irate customer is a very good thing even if it can be painful.

4 COLLECTING TESTIMONIALS

I've advised never to bribe a customer into giving a testimonial. Without bribery, why would anyone ever be willing to spend their time to help you sell your product? It turns out there are several reasons that a customer might help you.

The first reason, and the one that people most often admit to publicly, is to help their company. A testimonial carries weight specifically because the customer seems credible. In order to paint the customer giving the testimonial as credible, you need to say a little bit about them as part of the story.

This type of background story is good publicity for them. Even though it is part of your testimonial, it includes information about their company and what they do. It paints them in a good light since they talk about how they had a problem and were able to solve it with the use of your product or service. It makes them seem smart and pro-active.

The basic questions you want to answer in your testimonial about the target customer include:

- **Who** are they?
- **What** do they do?
- **What** were their challenges?
- **How** did they overcome them to improve their own operations?

All the promotion you do using their testimonial is advertising for them as well. And if you post the testimonial on your website or other promotional platform or product, you will most likely have some links back to the customer's web page. More links, higher search rankings. Add in the publicity, and what's not to like? It costs the customer very little in time, *and* they get free publicity.

If you are working with a customer who is in a group other than marketing, think about bringing in their marketing department. They will probably be a lot more eager to provide the testimonial because it equates to free publicity for them.

The next reason, which people think about but usually don't mention publicly, is that the individual giving the testimonial is also getting personal publicity. This helps the individual to be more widely known in the industry, and that certainly helps when it comes time to find a new job.

Finally, there is always the individual's ego. By asking them to give you a testimonial, you are acknowledging that they are recognized as a credible source for such a testimonial. It makes them feel important and brings them personal publicity which can only help their career (and ego).

Segmentation

When targeting stories for use to help attract prospective customers, it is important to make sure that the prospect will identify with the situation and customer. This may mean that you need to have several different groups of testimonials, with each one targeted at a different market segment.

You will need to carefully consider what the key characteristics are of your target market. Consider what characteristics are important to your customers. How do they identify themselves? What do they believe identifies their specific industry? There are many ways to look at the same business so it is important that you find out how they view themselves, not how you view them.

Testimonials do not have to be exactly the same in all aspects, but it is important to determine what characteristics your prospective customers will identify with. You want the prospective customers to look at the company detailed in the testimonial and be able to see themselves in that same situation.

This is another area where you can use the customer's own marketing department to help you. For starters, how do they describe themselves on their web site and in their promotional material? If it's not clear, give them a call and ask! Hopefully you are already talking to their marketing department anyway.

Some of the parameters that you may want to consider when developing your segmentation include the following.

- **Industry:** can your prospects identify with the use of your product in another industry?
- **Company size:** are you targeting large corporations, start-ups, mid-sized companies, etc.?
- **Geography:** are you targeting a multinational, or a company located primarily in one specific region that has its own characteristics?
- **Audience:** are you targeting executives, managers, engineers?
- **Job function:** do people in different jobs use your product in similar or different ways?

In addition to making sure that the customers you feature in your testimonials resonate with new prospects, you might also want to consider whether you need to have a range of use cases in your testimonials. If your customers are interested in hammers both to pound nails AND to pull nails out and you only have testimonials about pounding nails then they might not be satisfied that you can meet all their needs.

The Components of a Testimonial

A testimonial is a picture of how a customer was able to achieve their objectives through the use of your product. In a testimonial, you should not assume that the viewer or reader has any prior knowledge of your product. The main parts of a good testimonial should include the following:

- **Overview:** a short summary of the situation, problem, solution, results
- **Situation/background:** what the customer is developing and what their market is
- **Problem/pain statement:** what problem the customer was looking for a solution to
- **Reason for selecting your product:** what was attractive to them and what expectations they had for a solution
- **Results/impact:** what changed, what quantitative metrics they saw, how was the problem solved
- **Conclusion:** recap and call-to-action

There may be special cases where you omit one of these sections but those are unusual. In most cases these are going to be the six key sections of an effective testimonial. Let's look at them a little closer.

The **overview** is the most important section because you will run into people who really don't want to read the whole thing. It's important to give them the key information right up front in case that's all they read. In addition, if you lay out your case in the first few sentences then you might encourage them to keep reading or watching.

The **situational background** is where the customer gets to promote their company, and also where the reader begins to identify with the customer.

The **problem statement** is the second half of the identification process. With this, the reader now is hopefully thinking, "Yes, I'm just like that company and I have those same problems."

The **reason for selecting your product** is important because that lends credibility to the use of your product. It's good that the customer used you, but why did they use you? Where you the only solution for this problem? Where you the best? Where you the most reliable company to do business with? What makes you the right pick?

Note that this is more than just offering an example; you are ideally going to do the reader's work for them here. They need to go through the exact same process in their own evaluation, and this is your chance to guide their thinking here by providing them with an answer.

The **results** section is obviously important because it says that your product does what you say it does. If you have actual statistics and they are impressive you should include them. "The product improved productivity by 106%" or "The product let us do our work in 46% of the regular time" or "We improved profits by 372%".

You want to be careful about numbers here. If you did improve their results but only by 10% you might want to just stick with 'Improved results" unless in your industry a 10% gain is a big deal. The point is that numbers are always best unless they are not actually impressive, and then you usually want to stick with "better", "faster", "higher", etc.

Finally, the **conclusion** should quickly re-iterate the key points of the testimonial and leave the reader with a call-to-action. As the saying goes, you want to tell the reader what you are going to tell them, then tell them, then tell them what you just told them. It sounds redundant but it works.

The final **call-to-action** does not need to be complex but don't make them guess what to do next. Even if it's as simple as "Call us now at 123-456-7890" or "Go to xyz.com for more information" you always want to tell them what to do. It's one of those little tiny steps where you just help guide them along the path.

Never make your prospect work when you can guide them. If you give them the testimonial and just stop there then the customer has to make that extra step of thinking, "Huh, maybe they could do that for me - maybe I should call them." It's a small thing but driving a customer to buy is often made up of a series of small things that all add up to a purchase.

Now that we know what to put in a testimonial, how do we collect the content that we need to build the testimonial? The heart of the testimonial is the customer interview.

The Interview

The best interview is one recorded on video. With video endorsements, you can create stories, add other audio layers, and then mine the conversation to provide print versions as well. Video can raise the price tag quite a bit, however, and the customer may not agree to that format anyway.

If you are not recording video, then the next best thing is a live, in-person interview. This allows the interviewer to read body language and get a better feel for how to follow up on specific answers. If the interviewer is not local to the customer and travel is not feasible, then a phone interview can be done, but it will be less effective. A video conference call is a good compromise, if possible.

Whether in person or over the phone, it is best to always record the interview instead of just taking notes by hand. Remember that in most states, this cannot be done legally without the interviewee's knowledge and consent, and if they say no, then that means no. Even if you and the customer are in states where it is legal to record without everyone's knowledge, it can upset the customer if you don't tell them and they find out later. Don't risk it; always ask.

As long as you explain that you only want to make sure you don't miss anything or misquote them, people rarely object. From your perspective as the interviewer, having to manually take notes during the conversation is distracting and will keep the conversation from flowing easily. On the other hand, you will get an opportunity to review your notes with the customer later, so it's not a disaster if you have to take notes by hand, just not preferable.

You definitely want to have a complete set of questions written out in advance, and you should send these to the customer ahead of time for them to think about. Note, however, that few people will write about as much detail as they will talk about, and so it is rarely advisable to let the customer simply reply with a text response to the list of questions.

You will gain much more information and be able to pursue any unexpected areas of information if you are having a live conversation with the customer. It's okay to follow up with a few quick questions by email, but the initial interview should be done live.

The only exception is where you and the customer do not speak the same language, or one of you speaks it so poorly that it is difficult to understand. In this situation a live interview is actually not better than an email exchange.

The Interviewer

A good customer testimonial can be written by anyone, but there is real value in having a professional writer create the story for you.

Here you may have to make some trade-offs, but ideally you want to use someone who is a professional writer, who has experience interviewing people and writing customer testimonials, and who has at least some understanding of your industry.

If you don't have someone with all of those qualifications in your company, it may be money well spent to hire a consultant with the right background to conduct the interview and write the story. If there really is a problem with the industry knowledge being critical, you can have an insider conduct the interview (with or without the writer on the phone) and then have a consultant write the story.

Finding Approval

With many customer testimonials, the most difficult part of the process can be obtaining permission from the customer's company. Some large companies have blanket policies against providing any endorsements, viewing it both as a dilution of their own brand by association with your product and as a possible disclosure of practices that are part of the company's proprietary competitive advantages. Indeed, I have worked with several large, well-known companies that have this proprietary attitude. Naturally, I can't tell you who they are!

Unfortunately, these large companies are the ones that carry the most influence. An endorsement from IBM is far more valuable than one from Joe's Computer Start-up. Customer testimonials from small companies are still valuable, especially if they are recognized as doing something leading-edge themselves, but the larger the recommending company and therefore the better known the name, the better off you are.

One way to help get approval through a legal process where your testimonial is far from a priority to them is to engage the customer's marketing department in helping your cause. A testimonial is a way of promoting your product, true, but it also shows the customer in a positive light (because they were successful), and it is a way to talk about some new product or technology that they have developed. Everywhere that you promote that particular testimonial, you are promoting not only your company but theirs as well.

You can often find a valuable ally on the customer side by talking to the people who are responsible for marketing whatever product is described in the story. It's a way of promoting their product, and having a marketing manager champion the story internally because it will help promote their product is a far better push than simply having the end user justify it because they are doing you (their vendor) a favor.

One final note on approval: the best time to secure the agreement to do the testimonial is during the negotiation for the original sale. If the customer asks for discount, include the testimonial as a condition of the discount. This ties an actual cost saving for the customer to the completion of the testimonial. This makes it compelling for the end user who is giving you the actual quotes and for the internal teams that will need to approve the story.

5   VIDEO TESTIMONIALS: DOING IT RIGHT

Nothing beats video for impact, especially for a customer testimonial. A video interview shows us that a real person made the comments, and we always feel a little more comfortable when we can see the person and make a judgment about their credibility based on whether they seem to be enthusiastic or at least confident in what they are saying.

The best way to create a video testimonial is to hire a local video crew to record the interview and then edit the video down to the two minutes or so that seems to be the most effective length to maintain viewer interest. Yes, this costs money, but do you want a useful and credible product in the end or something that looks like an amateur home video? The latter may be easy on your budget, but it certainly does not make your company look very professional.

Prices vary widely depending on location and other logistics, but you can expect to spend roughly $2,000 for a full-day crew rental, and about another $1,000 for editing. The editing can vary quite a bit depending on how good the interviewee was, how much footage the contractor needs to edit, and how many iterations you make with the editor.

A basic video crew is going to consist of a primary camera operator and one or two assistants. You will always want a two-camera setup so you have something to jump between to make it more interesting and easier to edit. You may or may not need additional lighting, but the crew you hire should certainly bring it. Basically, if they do not show up with a cart loaded with equipment, you've hired the wrong group.

In most teams, the two people will work the two cameras during recording, or sometimes one person will manage both cameras and the second person will focus on sound. I prefer the latter approach because sound is actually the most important part of a video. You can fix spotty video (to an extent); you can't fix bad sound. In a three-person setup, you will usually have one person on each camera, and the third person will monitor the sound recording.

You do not want one person running a two-camera setup if you can afford the money. With lighting and sound added in, that's just too much for one person to monitor without risking the quality of the results. If you have gone to all the trouble to line up the customer, and possibly travel there for the interview, saving a few dollars and risking the entire shoot is just not worth it. On the other hand, if you get a quote for much more than $2,000, you are also talking to the wrong people.

I highly recommend hiring a crew unless you happen to have one in your company. If you absolutely have no choice, you certainly can record the customer yourself as well as conduct the interview, but with several caveats. The first is that you may need to reshoot the whole interview. Since you are not monitoring the cameras fully while you conduct the interview, it is very important to check the footage you shot right after recording.

If something went wrong, or the audio was distorted, or the sun moved and shadowed the subject—or a million other things that can happen—you will need to reshoot the interview. If you have a super friendly customer with not much else to do that day, you might be able to get away with that. This will usually not be the case, though.

Everyone is a videographer today. People use their phones to record things on the spot and then upload to YouTube, Facebook, TikTok, or any number of platforms. But most of these do look like they were recorded by someone with their phone. Video recording and editing can be as complicated as you want it to be, but for what you are trying to accomplish here, it is possible to get away with the basics.

Once again, I highly encourage you to hire a professional videographer to shoot and edit your testimonial videos. If it's worth recording a customer talking about you, it's worth doing it right. If you just don't have the budget for that, it is still possible to do it yourself. The quality won't be as high, and you run the risk of making a mistake that leaves you with unusable video, but it is cheaper.

6 SHOOTING YOUR OWN VIDEO

There are entire books written in detail on each individual aspect of shooting video and I'm only going to give you an overview here. This should at least get you started and headed in the right direction. One critical tip: you should try shooting and editing a few videos with friends or co-workers and going all the way through the flow before you take it out on the road and work with a real customer.

Audio

The first and most important thing to consider is sound. People will forgive a lot of faults with the video, but not with the audio. Nothing screams *unprofessional* more than bad sound. Fortunately, this is easy to correct, and the first way to fix this is to never use the built-in microphone on whatever you are using for a camera.

Built-in microphones (mics) suffer from two main problems: they are compromised by being general purpose, and since they are physically on the camera they are too far away from the speaker. A built-in microphone is designed to pick up all sound in the room, only part of which is what your speaker is saying. This makes the audio noisy, and it distracts from the speaker. To fix this you need to get the microphone off the camera and use an external mic that you plug into the camera.

There are two main types of microphones commonly used for fixing the audio: a **shotgun mic** or a **lavalier (lav) mic**.

A **shotgun mic** is designed to pick up sound from a very narrow space. It shuts out sound from everywhere else in the room. Because it is not physically attached to the camera, you can also get this mic in closer to the speaker, which further helps make the speaker louder than any surrounding noise.

The second option is to use a **lavalier mic**. This is a small mic that clips onto the speaker's shirt, typically with the mic cable running under the shirt and around the back. You've seen these on talk shows, game shows, and many other TV productions. It's small, but you can still see it clipped to the speaker's shirt, dress, or jacket.

The **shotgun mic** has the advantage of not requiring the speaker to be set up to wear a mic, and it is not visible on the camera. The downside is that the mic needs to be placed close to and pointed directly at the speaker but just out of the camera's view.

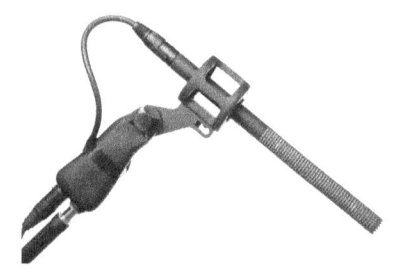

You can't take any wide shots of the room when using a shotgun mic because of the need to have the mic close to the audio source (the speaker), although that might not be a problem. Lavalier mics are small and will not get in the way, but the speaker does have to be wired.

The first characteristic to consider about any microphone is whether its output is **high impedance** or **low impedance**. It's not important for you to know exactly what that means but rather how they are used. Low-impedance microphones are more professional: they are lower noise, and you can have longer cables connecting the microphone to the camera. High-impedance microphones are used for consumer equipment, they are often noisier (depending on the environment), and you shouldn't use long cables.

Low-impedance mics are easily identified by the larger, round connecter that has three pins inside. High-impedance microphones use connectors that are of a more familiar style, like what you would use to plug into your iPhone or, in a slightly larger form, a guitar amplifier. Lower-end video cameras and DSLR (digital single lens reflex) cameras will usually have high-impedance connectors.

Professional cameras (or "pro-sumer" which are half-way between PROfessional and conSUMER categories) will usually have low-impedance inputs and sometimes also support high-impedance, too. For your purposes, the less expensive high-impedance microphones will usually be fine, but in either case make sure that the camera you have supports the type of mic you have.

Having said that, if you go the cheaper high-impedance route, you want to get a top-of-the-line high-impedance mic. You can get a $10 mic, but it will probably sound bad and be very noisy. Again, try out all your equipment before you use it in a real interview. High-impedance lavalier mics will run from $10 to $100 on average. Low-impedance mics can run from $100 to $1,000.

Another factor to consider is the use of wired versus wireless microphones. A wireless lavalier microphone uses a small wireless transmitter the size of a pack of cards, usually worn by the speaker. This allows the speaker to move about without any visible wire running from the microphone to the camera. For the purpose of an interview, this is almost always an unnecessary complication and expense. Stick with the wired models and you have one less thing to go wrong.

Lighting

The next thing to consider is the lighting. Good lighting can make a huge difference. Can you just use room light? Yes, in a pinch, but overhead lights are designed to light up your work surfaces, not your face. You can get odd shadows on the face from the overheads, and uneven lighting.

Lighting a speaker directly so that they are better lit than the background helps make them stand out from their surroundings. If the walls behind the speaker are lit to the same degree as (or even more than) the speaker, it will make the person less distinct visually.

The ideal lighting setup is called three-point lighting because it uses three lights at three different points around the subject. There is one main light in front of the speaker and slightly to one side. This is called the key light. A second, less powerful light is set up also in front but on the other side and is called a fill light because it fills in the shadows. Finally, a third light is positioned above and behind the speaker and is called a back light.

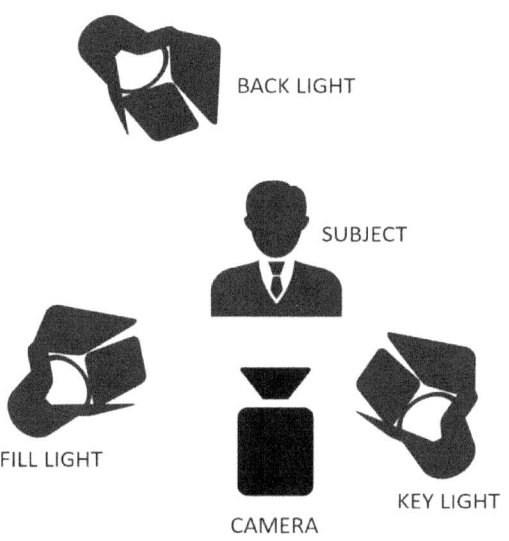

Fig 1 – Three-point lighting

Why do we need all of these? Why not just the one in the middle?

Having a single light in the middle—or at least at the same angle as the camera—doesn't give any visible shadows and it makes the face look very flat. Pulling the one key light around at an angle to the speaker now creates more depth, but often too much depth due to the sharp shadows cast by the one light. With two or three point lighting, the key light lights up one side of the speaker's face, and the fill light lights up the other side.

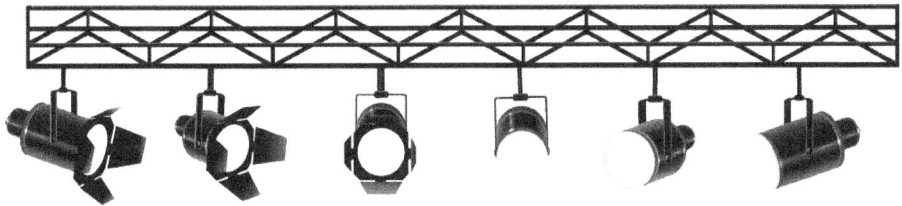

However, you generally don't want both lights to be the same brightness because that renders a less interesting visual effect. Having two lights with one brighter makes one side of the face lighter and gives you some more depth to the video. Only using a key light on one side makes the other side of the face darker and is more of an artistic look, which is less common in an interview.

The third light (the back-light) helps light up the head and shoulders from the back and makes the speaker stand out more from the background. If you don't have a back-light try to make sure that the background is not the same color as the hair or shirt of the subject.

If you only have one light to work with, you can compromise and have the key light at a slight angle to the speaker. This will help give some light to both sides of the face but still provide some "depth" by lighting one side more than the other.

Complicating all of this are the lights that are in the room to begin with. The best scenario is where you can turn off all the room lights, block any windows, and only use the light from your lighting setup. Unfortunately, this is not always possible. Sometimes you will have room lights that can't be turned off, or you might have to contend with windows and daylight with no curtains. If you have to deal with these, you can also run into problems with light color, referred to as *temperature*.

Incandescent lights have more red in their light; daylight has more blue. Fluorescent lights can tend toward either, depending on the bulbs used. If you have a light kit that has a color temperature to match incandescent light, and you also have daylight in the room, the speaker's skin can be lit with different colors in different places. Likewise, if you have daylight temperature lights and the room has incandescent lights, you can also get patches of mismatched skin tones.

Fortunately, LED light panels have largely replaced the heavier, hotter lighting of the past, and one of the extra benefits of LED lighting is that it is easy to include two different color LEDs in the array. A switch or dial lets you adjust the individual lights to match daylight or incandescent lights. These lights range from several hundred dollars on the low end to several thousand on the high end. The more expensive lights are brighter, sturdier, and have more precise control. For your purposes, you can usually go with the less expensive lights.

Cameras

Contrary to what you might think, for our purposes the camera is really the least important piece of equipment. With good sound and good lighting, even consumer grade cameras can give you reasonable results for videos that will be posted on the web and mostly watched in small, low-resolution windows.

Keep in mind that your target is not a movie screen but a small video on part of a website or a video platform like YouTube. This does not mean that you should strive to use a poor camera, but don't stress not being able to afford a nice $5,000 professional unit either.

The first choice is to pick either a traditional video camera or to use a DSLR. The DSLRs were originally designed for still pictures, but they quickly added video capabilities, while video cameras also added functionality to take still pictures so today there is some overlap.

Dedicated video cameras have extra features that make them better for shooting video, and DSLRs have features that make them better for still photography. If you are only going to be using the camera for occasional videos, a DSLR might be a better all-around camera for you.

The next question is whether to use one or two cameras. A normal interview will use at least two, at slightly different angles and with one zoomed in closer than the other. This gives you two different views to cut back and forth between during the interview. This is more visually interesting than simply having a single, still camera for the entire interview, but more importantly it is used to disguise the editing.

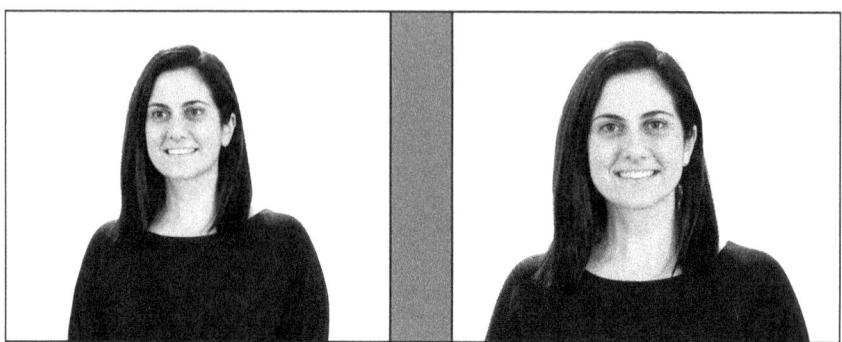

Fig 2 – Two-camera shot with two angles

When you edit out a section of the interview, either because the speaker said something that was not important or it doesn't fit in with the theme, there will be a noticeable jump in the video when it cuts between the two segments. This is covered, however, by jumping from one camera shot to the other in order to disguise the cut.

The best way to use two cameras is to have one—usually the front camera—focused in on just the subject's face, and have the second camera at a slight angle with a wider focus. This lets you cut to a closeup shot of the subject to emphasize specific points, and then cut to a wider shot to give perspective.

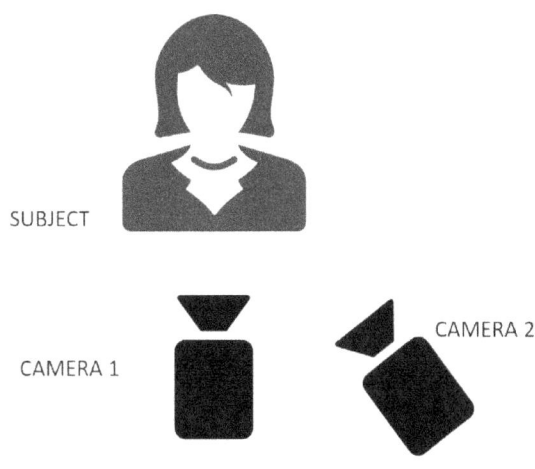

Fig 3 – Two-camera setup

When only one camera is used, you can still disguise the cut by zooming in a bit to create what seems like a second-camera shot. This gives you two shots to cut between: one full-frame and one zoomed in a bit.

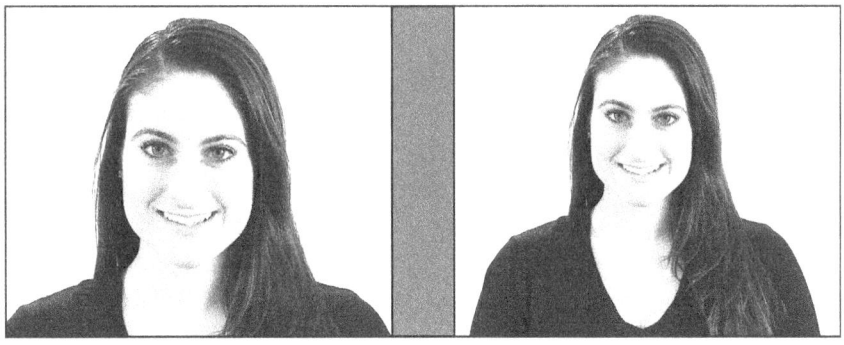

Fig 4 – One-camera shot with zoom

This is not as interesting as cutting between two different camera angles, but it's better than just having a series of jarring jumps in the final edit.

One final note is that you must use a tripod to hold the camera steady. For these purposes, however, it doesn't matter what kind of tripod you have, and it need not be an expensive one.

Where to Shoot

The background is very important. Changing weather, traffic, or other motion limit your ability to edit later without having the picture look very jumpy, which is distracting. If you absolutely have to have mobile elements in the background like people, try to get people to make comments in one continuous speech so you can minimize editing later.

Pick a background that is darker than your subject. A well-lit background can skew the contrast on your camera, and the person you are trying to shoot will end up too dark. Even if you are able to adjust the contrast, you will end up with a background that is overexposed. On top of that, it is distracting to have brighter things than your subject visible in the frame.

Likewise, try to get some light on your subject. If you are at a conference, you are probably going to be working with an array of overhead lights and not have much flexibility. If you have any control at all, try to make sure there is some light on your subject's face and not a lot of light on the background.

Taking Your Time

Don't be in a hurry. Slow down; take your time; get it right. Rushing is never good, especially when you are conducting an impromptu video shoot with no planning. And make sure to give yourself plenty of raw video to work with later.

Don't hit the record button and immediately say *Go*. Digital memory is cheap. Start recording, wait a second or two, then start asking your questions. Likewise, when the subject is done speaking, let the video go for a few more seconds, and then stop recording. There is nothing quite so frustrating as realizing later that you ruined a perfect quote because you cut off half of the first or last word.

Editing

Once you have recorded the video, you need to edit it. There are several video-editing tools available that are reasonably priced and easy to use. As with cameras, the high-end video-editing tools provide far more functionality than you will ever need and are harder to use.

Why do you need to edit? For starters, you want to cut down the interview to just the one to two minutes of highlights and key messages. Any longer than two minutes will lose most viewers. You might also want to add some music or some intro graphics, perhaps even just your logo. This is not hard to do and will not require learning a complicated editing tool.

Editing is a whole other topic. If you are going edit your own videos, pick the editor that seems most attractive to you. Spend some time with the editor utility going through any tutorials or other examples. Take some older footage from a previous interview and practice editing it down. Most editing software has free trial periods.

Once you understand how NLEs (non-linear editors) work, you have the fundamentals down. Each editor, however, will have its own little quirks that you will need to learn. The good news is that modern editors are so full featured that, for your purposes, you will only be using about 5 percent of the editor's functionality, if that.

7 USING SMARTPHONES

Smartphones have turned everyone into videographers. While they are getting better each year, smartphones are still not the best cameras. Under the right circumstances you can get good video with a smartphone, and there have even been entire movies shot using a smartphone. But they are still very limited in their ability and using one makes life more challenging.

However, if you remember a few simple tips you can at least shoot better video using a smartphone or other small, consumer-level camera.

- Use **a tri-pod** to keep the phone steady
- Find a spot that has **good lighting**
- Use an **external microphone**

Let's look at these in some more detail.

Smooth and Steady

The first thing to remember is to keep the shot steady. You don't absolutely have to use a tripod but you do need to keep the camera reasonably steady. You are not going to pass this off as a professional video, so it is okay to have some movement that shows you are holding the camera in your hand. If you don't think you can hold it reasonably steady, then try bracing your arm against a table, pillar, or anything stable.

You can buy little tripod adaptors that clamp onto a smartphone, if that's more desirable; coupled with a small tabletop tripod, you can get steady shots. But this assumes that you walk around every day with a mini tripod in your pocket just waiting for those unexpected opportunities.

Part of keeping it steady means not whipping your camera around to show what else is going on. If you absolutely have to show something else or look at what the person is talking about, then do it later when your subject is not speaking (or whatever they are doing). Waving your camera around will make the audience seasick and give you unusable video. If you want to show multiple things, show them with multiple shots.

No digital zoom. Ever! Digital zooms work by reducing the camera resolution. This is bad and will render your video unusable. Never do anything to reduce the quality of the raw video you are shooting. You might decide you want to do something like that later when editing, but for now just focus on getting the best possible video you can.

In fact, no zoom of any kind should be used. Even if you have an optical zoom on your phone (and you probably don't), your chance of using it effectively and not making the video look odd is slim. And if you are so far away from your subject that you want to zoom in on them, then you are probably too far away, and the audio is going to be bad.

Finding the Light

Of course there is no reason why you can't use actual pro lights with a smartphone but if you are using a smartphone as a camera it's probably because you don't have the budget for a real camera which means you probably don't have the budget for lights.

In that case, just remember the important points about lighting. Do not just use an overhead light to provide light. That will cast odd shadows on your subject. Try to find a place to shoot your video where there is light mostly in front of the subject and not as much overhead.

One trick you can try it so have the subject facing a white wall, and have an overhead light just behind them. This will give them some backlight and will also bounce off the wall to provide some front lighting. Conversely, having a subject up against a wall in a large room filled with overhead lighting will provide a bank of lights that are somewhat in front of them.

Try to pick a room that has either overhead light or natural light from a window, but not a mix of both. Remember that these two light sources have different color temperatures.

Finally, if you are using natural lighting beware of changing light because of clouds or the sun moving while you shoot. Nothing looks more disconcerting than having the light changing visibly during the edited video.

Smartphone Audio

Again, I cannot stress enough how important sound is. This is not something you can fudge and fix later. Good audio is far more important than good video. A good interview could be set to a picture or series of pictures and not use the original video. Good video with poor audio is useless. You need good quality sound and no disrupting noise.

If you are at a noisy conference, try to at least find a less noisy corner to conduct the interview in. But not something like a stairwell—that will just look weird and often have excessive echo. Most importantly, you need to get as close as possible to the subject. Get right in their face. This will get you better video and much better sound. The audio will be clearer, and the ratio of voice to background noise will be better.

Most phones have some way of using an external audio source. This will be either through a combined headphone/mic jack or via Bluetooth. In some more recent phones, you might only have a Bluetooth connection available. You can plug a low-impedance, wired lavalier mic into your phone, just as you would with a dedicated camera, and this can give you fairly good audio.

CUSTOMER TESTIMONIALS FOR FUN AND PROFIT

You can even buy a mini shotgun mic that plugs into your phone. This won't give you as good a soundtrack as a wired lavalier, but it will definitely give you better audio than using the built-in mic, and you don't have to clip a mic on the subject.

Those are a few points to remember when using a smartphone or other low-end camera to try to capture video. It will probably never be great video, but if you are careful, you can end up with good video.

8 CONFERENCE & TRADE-SHOW INTERVIEWS

One venue that deserves special highlighting is the trade show or conference. In-depth interviews are nice, but you can usually get several shorter ones more easily. The end result is almost the same: prospects get to see and hear your customers giving you a recommendation. You can set up a separate booth or meeting area dedicated to recording the interviews, or you can just make it a part of your booth and use a corner of your space when you have someone to talk to.

You will want someone to act as an interviewer. This person will usually not be on camera, but you could do your interviews in a news-interview format where both the interviewer and interviewee are on camera. Even if the interviewer is not visible, you will want someone asking questions and prompting the customer. For effective material, never just stick a camera in someone's face and tell them to talk!

You will also need to have a set of questions prepared in advance. Even if you pursue something the customer said and go off script, you will still want a set to start from. Ideally, you should give the questions to the customer before you interview them. This can mean handing them the questions written out or just reviewing them first.

This will help the customer be prepared and more comfortable during the interview—and may even encourage them to agree to the interview in the first place. If you start off by saying that you want to interview them and you are going to ask them x, y, and z questions, they will feel more comfortable with the idea than if the process is unknown.

One way to make the process easier is to organize the questions around a single topic or theme. Telling a prospective interviewee that you would like to ask them some questions about topic x gives you a more natural entry into a conversation. That may be the overall video theme, or it may be a particular aspect of what you want to cover.

In fact, you might not want to talk to people directly about your product at all. You can get some useful video of having customers and prospects talking about the problems that they are facing—problems that, of course, your product can solve!

By now you may be wondering if you are going to be able to get people to agree to be interviewed in an impromptu setting. This is not at all a given, and you can't expect people to simply stop what they are doing and take time out of their conference agenda to let you record them. But there are ways to encourage them.

As with any other customer interview, this is something that you will use to promote your product, but it is also a chance for your customer to get some publicity as well. Giving them a chance to introduce themselves and their business will promote their product or service each time you use the video.

This applies to individuals as well as the product: you may be promoting their company, but you are also promoting them personally. This may more readily convince them to participate than pitching it as just something to help their company.

One way to make it easier to land interview subjects is to schedule them all before the show. It will require some extra time to set up, but it also gives you more time to talk them into saying they'll do it—and committing to it. They may be more inclined to say yes before they are actually at the show and surrounded by distractions.

You will still have the advantage of being able to talk to many customers in one place at one time, but you'll be working with less uncertainty. The flip side, however, is that by asking them at the conference with no advance notice, you give them less time to be nervous and have second thoughts about participating.

Naturally, it is going to be obvious on the video that you are talking to people at a trade show. Even under the best circumstances, there will be some background noise from the environment that you can't eliminate. However, you can use this to your advantage by working this into the interviews. Make the show part of the story.

You can start by announcing that you are at the x show talking to y, and then show some background video of the exterior of the venue and the activity at the trade show or conference. Just make sure you check with the event management about the rules for video recording and be mindful of who appears in the video if you don't have signed release forms.

9 RELEASE FORMS

Speaking of which… And this is extremely important, so I'm devoting a whole short chapter on this topic alone. Make sure that anyone you interview signs a release form. In fact, make sure anyone that is on camera at all, even in the background, signs a release form.

There are situations where you don't need release forms for everyone but play it safe and always get them. You can easily find sample release forms online or ask your lawyer to make one up for your specific usage.

I am not going to include one here because I'm not a lawyer and I'm not qualified to give legal advice. However, I can give you the advice that you need legal advice. That much I am qualified for.

But do you *really* need a release form? Is anyone going to ever actually care? In all likelihood, no. I have conducted a lot of customer interviews and I've never had a problem arise where I had to produce the release form to prove we had permission.

I've also never had my house burn down, but you can believe that I have house insurance. It's easy to do, and it protects you in the unlikely event that something happens. Don't get sloppy, get a release.

If you are scheduling an on-site interview, make sure you send the release form along with the questions ahead of time. Some companies will want their own lawyer to review the release, and they might want changes made. You are investing a lot of time and money to do an on-site interview, so you want to make sure there are no glitches.

By contrast, in an impromptu interview setting I usually have people sign the release form afterwards. Yes, they might then get cold feet and not sign it, but most people will feel obligated to sign it after having just completed the recording. The worst case in this situation is that you'll have only lost five to ten minutes if they say no.

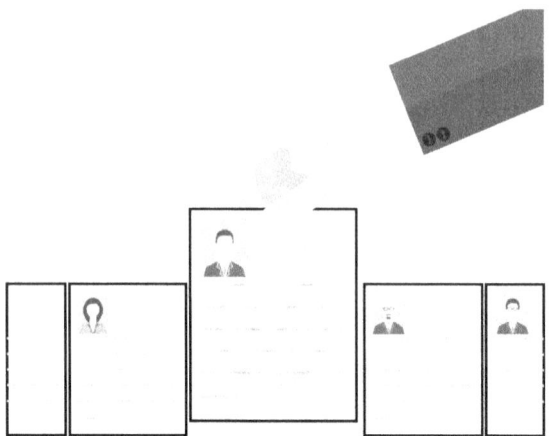

10 USING THE TESTIMONIALS

Customer testimonials are only useful if your prospects actually watch or read them. Don't just post them on your website and wait for someone to find them or wait for the sales team to provide a link to them during a sales call. Use them to actually drive lead generation by publicizing them widely.

Magazines (print and online) love customer case studies, and this is a great way to get them in front of many prospects at once. Many people love searching YouTube for relevant content. Utilize all avenues for publication that you have: newsletters, blogs, articles, social network platforms—whatever is appropriate to reach your particular customer base.

Format and Targets

When a customer provides you with enough material to record or write a testimonial and has agreed to work with you to develop it, you should make the most use of this material that you can. An interview for a testimonial can be mined for a wide variety of uses. Quotes can be extracted from the interview and used on websites, in presentations, for advertisements, on banners at trade shows…pretty much anywhere.

You can write a press release about the customer's successful use of your product. You can take the interview, possibly with some follow-up detail, and write an application note on that customer's specific usage. The material can be used to create an article or blog post on the success of the customer's project, which happens to use your product.

Keep in mind that most magazine or blog editors want to hear primarily about what the customer did, not about how wonderful your product is, so the focus in an article will need to be different unless you want to pay for it as an advertisement.

YouTube

The most popular place to post a video is YouTube. The service is free, it's easy to use, and you get extra promotion from search results if you tag it correctly and employ best practices for SEO. YouTube offers good analytics, so you know exactly who is watching and when and for how long. While there are other video hosting services, YouTube is the 800-pound gorilla, so to speak…or maybe even the 8,000-pound gorilla.

There are, however, some drawbacks to YouTube. Perhaps most importantly, you can't change the video once it's been posted. If you do need to change it, you need to post the new version and get a new link to it. The original link cannot be updated. For something like a customer testimonial, this is rarely a problem.

In most cases, you are not going to go back and re-edit a testimonial. If you do, you can just post it as a new video with the new focus. The only real problem with not being able to update a video is if you later decide that some of the messaging or comments are actually wrong or problematic. In that case, you want to not only create a new video but also remove the old one.

If you have heavily promoted the original video, then lots of sources have the link to the original video that will now go nowhere. Deciding that a testimonial was so off that it was actually wrong and needs to be taken down is extremely unusual, and if that is ever the case you probably have bigger problems than just your video.

Posting a video directly on your web page does ensure that the viewer will have access to lots of other content that supports your promotion. Of course, you can embed a YouTube video into your web page as well (which most people do), and on the YouTube page you can always include links to your web page.

CUSTOMER TESTIMONIALS FOR FUN AND PROFIT

One thing that is important to note is that there is currently no way to disable the view counts on a YouTube video. This means that everyone will see how many people have watched your video. Nothing is more embarrassing and tells everyone that nobody cares about you and your product than having videos with a very small view count.

Once you post a video and are ready to promote it on YouTube, you need to make sure that you get the view count at least over 100 or much more depending on the normal size of your audience. If you sell a rare specialty product, 100 views might be a lot. If you are Apple and you have a video about your new iPhone, 100 would be an utter failure.

Once you figure out what normal engagement looks like for your product's niche, make sure you get those views right away. There are services where you can buy views, and you need to be a little careful with those. YouTube does look for suspicious view bumps and can drop the views if they trigger a fake-views alert.

More importantly, make sure you don't have a ridiculously large number of views which also looks odd. If your market is only a few thousand people and you suddenly have 10,000 views, that's going to look as wrong as only having ten views. The easiest way to get your first round of views is simply to have everyone in your company watch the video a few times – from their phone, from their laptop, etc..

If you are using a video for promotion, everyone in your company should watch the video anyway so they know what your customers are saying about you. If you need a bigger bump than that, have them all ask family and friends to watch as well.

Make a Landing Page

In addition to posting the video on YouTube or other hosting service, you should have a landing web page for the video. Not just a page with only the video, but one that supports the products or messages that the customer talks about.

If the customer talks about a specific product, have some information about that product on the page. If they discuss some specific application, have some more information about that application on that page.

If they refer to any kind of digital product that can be posted (data, reports, images, etc.), then have actual examples of those posted there. You can include links to the customer, their industry, or any other information about them.

The video is the centerpiece of the page, but the rest of the page should be filled with supporting information to make the story come alive even more and use the messages in the video as a springboard for deeper engagement with the viewer.

Hosting

If you do decide to host your video outside of YouTube, there are two main ways to go. First, you can simply place the final video file on your web server. That is the easiest, and it's free. But it's also very limited and means that you need to manually add in features that come for free with hosting services.

The other option is to use a video hosting service like Wistia, Brightcove, and others.

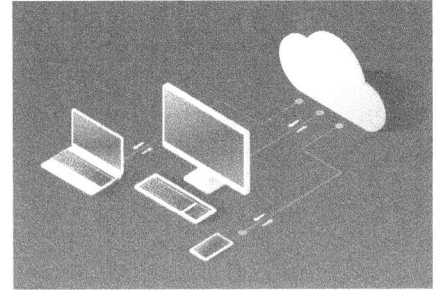

These video services can offer a number of features, including more detailed analytics, tighter integration with CRM systems, more control over presentation, and, of course, the ability to modify a video without losing the links.

Many people will opt to use both YouTube and a hosting service, and this can work out well if used correctly. Keep in mind that you will get some cannibalization between the two channels, which might not be a problem, but you will have to combine results and analysis to some extent. YouTube is better for reach and social interaction, no question.

One strategy that can be very effective is to post shorter intro or teaser videos on YouTube and then point back to your website for the longer version. That lets you engage in social media with a short video that fits in with the short attention span typically devoted to such channels, and it also serves to help separate the "tire kickers" from the serious prospects that should be followed up with.

The broader reach of YouTube-based videos are great for brand awareness, and the prospects who follow your links back to get more information on your website let you know who you should be engaging with right away.

Email

Of course, you are going to want to promote your new testimonial video, and certainly that means sending it out to everyone in your database. You should not to try to email the actual video itself, but you can include a description, a link, and an image from the video that will pique their interest.

Keep in mind that many people have email clients that do not automatically download images. You can have the most compelling image in your email that links to your video, yet many people will never see it.

Always make sure that when you use graphics, you also have enough text in your email to explain what the video is and why they should watch it. You want to be able to get your message across with the text and get them interested and comfortable enough to click on the link or at least download the images and see the visual content.

Integration with Sales/Marketing Automation Systems

Make it easy for sales personnel to send it out: create an email template in whatever sales or marketing automation system(s) you are using. Or even just create an email template that sales can use directly to fill out and send to prospects.

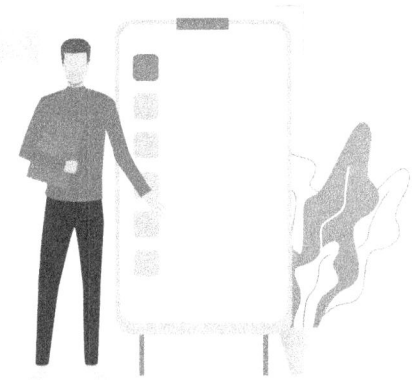

11 JUST DO IT

Customer testimonials are clearly very important. Not *Yes, when we get around it*–important, but rather *We must get this done*–important. Good testimonials can really help you sell your product, and their absence can really hurt your product's impression.

Getting your customers to say good things about you is not hard, but it can take perseverance and patience. It does help if lots of people actually like your product, but that is only the initial step. And while a straight up *Your company is wonderful* testimonial is your goal, even a short quote will go a long way to helping you establish credibility.

The single most important thing is that it has to actually be someone's job, or at least part of their stated goals, to get these customer testimonials done. I've seen too many cases where it was merely something that sales and marketing was supposed to do when they had the time or opportunity.

Guess what? It never gets done that way. It does take time and effort, and if it's not something that people will be rewarded for at review time…it won't happen.

The best situation is to have someone in your company whose job it is to actually gather customer testimonials. That way you know it's going to get done because it's actually their job and not item #26 on their job description.

Just don't forget that whoever is conducting the interview is going to need to know something about your product and your customers so they can ask intelligent and guiding questions. That might mean that you have one person responsible for getting the interview and setting it up, but you bring in a product expert to actually conduct the interview.

If you don't have the resources to dedicate someone to collecting testimonials, then at least make sure that it is included in people's objectives. And make it a real objective, not one that is included but ignored.

If you have a salesperson who has an objective of selling X amount of product and also to get 2 customer testimonials, guess which one is going to get 99.9% of their effort and which one is going to get 0.1% of their effort? And no one is going to care as long as they meet their sales quota.

That usually means that it needs to be an objective for someone in marketing. Here, too, don't just pile it on as an afterthought to get to when all the "important' things get done. Either make it a real objective, or just don't bother. A half-hearted attempt is just wasting everyone's time. As Yoda tells us, "Do or do not. There is no try."

I'll stop lecturing now but if you are still not convinced that you need customer testimonials then you haven't been paying attention. At the very least you should make it a priority to get a base set of testimonials and if you have to then let them age for a while at least you have something.

Ideally, however, you keep a regular stream of fresh testimonials coming so that you are not using the same three over and over for the next 5 years. Also you might have changes in product names, use models, or other issues that make an old testimonials sound dated. That kind of thing tends to stick out and be noticed.

I hope this has all helped give you some ideas about how to create and use customer testimonials. It's not hard to do, and it doesn't take a lot of time if you make sure that you include it in your Must Do pile on a regular basis. In the end, it can make a big difference and help you get one step ahead of your competition.

Happy hunting!

www.ingramcontent.com/pod-product-compliance
Lightning Source LLC
Chambersburg PA
CBHW051331220526
45468CB00004B/1592